Mudras for SCORPIO by SABRINA MESKO - 1

By Sabrina Mesko

Healing Mudras: Yoga for Your Hands – original edition
Power Mudras: Yoga Hand Postures for Women

CHAKRA MUDRAS DVD

HEALING MUDRAS
Yoga for Your Hands - New Edition

HEALING MUDRAS - new edition in full color:
Healing Mudras I. – For Your Body
Healing Mudras II. - For Your Mind
Healing Mudras III. – For Your Soul

MUDRA THERAPY
Hand Yoga for Pain Management and Conquering Illness

YOGA MIND
45 Meditations for Inner Peace, Prosperity and Protection

MUDRAS for ASTROLOGICAL SIGNS Series:

Mudras for ARIES
Mudras for TAURUS
Mudras for GEMINI
Mudras for CANCER
Mudras for LEO
Mudras for VIRGO
Mudras for LIBRA
Mudras for SCORPIO
Mudras for SAGITTARIUS
Mudras for CAPRICORN
Mudras for AQUARIUS
Mudras for PISCES

MUDRAS
for
SCORPIO

♏

By Sabrina Mesko Ph.D.H.

The material contained in this book has been written for
informational purposes and is not intended as a substitute
for medical advice nor is it intended to diagnose, treat,
cure, or prevent disease. If you have a medical issue or
illness, consult a qualified physician.

A Mudra Hands™ Book
Published by Mudra Hands Publishing

Photography by Mara
Animal photography by Sabrina Mesko
Illustrations by Kiar Mesko
Cover photo by Mara
Cover and interior book design by Sabrina Mesko
Printed in the United States of America

ISBN-13: 978-0615920931
ISBN-10: 0615920934

For all my Scorpio Friends

Table of Contents

With my Master Teacher Yogi Bhajan

Acknowledgments

I remain forever grateful to my Master Teacher Yogi Bhajan who entrusted me with bringing the ancient sacred Mudra techniques to a world wide audience.
The depictions of all Mudras in my literature have stayed true to his direction and approval.
Although I miss him dearly, He is with me forever in Spirit.

I have also had the fortune to personally learn about astrology from a few world renowned Indian Vedic Astrologers. I remain grateful for their knowledge and wisdom they so generously shared.

As always, my gratitude is to the One—the Universal power that has blessed me with gifts to share, challenges to overcome, lessons to learn, friends to cherish, love to spread, journeys to explore, moments of darkness to cherish the light, Wise men and Masters to teach me, luck to save me when needed, and my deep heartfelt desire to share all I've learned with You.

My thanks goes to my readers around the world who have shared with me their appreciation and the many benefits they experienced with Mudra practice.
I remain forever the humble instrument of the One.
May an abundance of blessings be with you now and always.

Mudras for SCORPIO

October 24 - November 22

BODY
SEXUAL ORGANS

PLANET
PLUTO

COLORS
DARK RED, MAROON

ELEMENT
WATER

STONES AND GEMS
OPAL

ANIMAL
INSECTS

Introduction

Ever since I can remember, I have been fascinated by the never ending view of the stars in the sky and the presence of other mysterious planets.
As a child I wondered for hours about where does the Universe end and when my Father explained the possibility that time and space exist in a very different way than we imagined, my mind went wild with possibilities.

I was however quite skeptical about astrology in general until one day in my early youth, a dear friend introduced me to a true Master of Vedic Astrology. He quickly and completely diminished any of my doubts about how precise certain facts can be revealed in one's Celestial map. It was as if an invisible veil had been removed, and I was granted a peek over to the other side. The astrologer also adamantly pointed out that nothing is written in stone and one's destiny has a lot of space to navigate thru. You can make the best of the situation if you know your given parameters.
My fascination and use of astrological science continues to this day and compliments and enriches my work with other observation techniques that I use when consulting.

One is born with character aspects and potential for realization of mapped-out future events, but there is always a possibility that another road may be taken. This has to do with the choices we make.
Free will is given to all of us, even though often the choices we have seem to be very limited. But still, the choices are always there, forcing us to consciously participate and eventually take responsibility for our decisions, actions, and consequences.

The science of Astrology has been around for millenniums and even though some people are still doubtful, I always remind them that there is no disputing the fact, that the Moon affects the high and low tide of our Oceans - hence our bodies consisting mostly of water are affected by planetary movements in many fascinating and profound ways. Even the biggest skeptic agrees with that fact.

The Love of the Universal Power for each one of us is unconditional, everlasting and omnipresent.
No matter what kind of life-journey you have, it is the very best one designed especially for you, rest assured.
And when you are experiencing life's various challenges and wishing for a smooth ride instead, keep in mind that a life filled with lessons is a life fulfilling its purpose. The tests you encounter in your daily life are your opportunities.
The wisdom learned is your asset, and the experiences gained are your wealth.
Your Spirit's abundance is measured by the battles you fought and how you fought them. Did you help others and leave this world a better place in any way? Your true intention matters more than you know.

Each one of us has a very unique-one of a kind celestial map placed gently, but firmly and irrevocably into effect at the precise time of our birth. There are certain aspects of one's chart that reveal possible character tendencies and predisposed behavior in regards to love, partnerships, maintaining one's health, pursuit of success and a way of communicating.

The benefits of knowing and understanding the effects of your chart on various aspects of your life can be profound. It can help you understand and prepare ahead of time for certain circumstances that are coming your way, which increases the possibility of a better quality of life in general.

If you knew that a specific time period could be beneficial for your career wouldn't it be good to know that ahead of your plans? If you are aware that certain aspects of your physical constitution are predisposed to a weakness or sensitivity, wouldn't it be beneficial to pay attention and prevent a possible future health ailment?

If you can foresee that a certain time will be slower for you in achieving positive results, wouldn't it be wise to use that time for preparation for a more fortuitous timing?

How many times have you attempted to pursue a dream of yours that just didn't seem to want to happen? And when you were completely exhausted and disillusioned, the fortunate opportunity presented itself, except now you were tired, overwhelmed and had no energy or enthusiasm left. Having such information ahead of time would offer you the chance to save your energy during quiet, less active time, so that when your luck is more likely, you can seize the opportunity and make the most of it.

Since writing my first books on Mudras a while ago, my work has expanded into many different areas, however I always included Mudras into my new ventures. When I designed International Wellness and Spa centers, I included Mudra programs to share these beneficial techniques with a wide audience. I included Mudras into my weekly TV show and guided large audiences thru practice on live shows.

Mudras will forever fascinate me and I have been humbled and excited how many practitioners from around the world have written me, grateful to have these techniques and most importantly really experiencing positive effects in time of need. Therefore it has been a natural idea for me to combine these two of my favorite topics and create a series of Mudra sets for all twelve Astrological signs.

The Mudras depicted in this book are specifically selected for the astrological sign of Scorpio with intention to help you maximize your gifts and soften the challenges that your celestial map contains.

It is important to know that each astrological chart - celestial map-contains information that can be used beneficially and there are no "bad signs" or "better sings". Your chart is unique as are you. By gaining information, knowledge and understanding what the placements of the planets offer you, your path to self knowledge is strengthened.

I hope this book will attract astrology readers as well as yoga practitioners and help you utilize the beneficial combination of both these fascinating techniques.

Knowledge will help you experience the very best possible version of your life. The biggest mystery in your life is You. Discover who you are and enjoy the journey.

And remember, no matter what life presents you with, don't forget to smile and keep a happy heart.

With each experience gained you are spiritually wealthier for it. And that my friend, stays with you forever.

The wisdom gained is eternally imprinted in your soul.

Blessings,

Sabrina

Mudras

Mudras are movements involving only fingers, hands and arms. Mudras originated in ancient Egypt where they were practiced by high priests and priestesses in sacred rituals. Mudras can be found in every culture of the world.

We all use Mudras in our everyday life when gesturing while communicating and when holding our hands in various intuitive positions.
Mudras used in yoga practice offer great benefits and have a tremendously positive overall effect on our overall state of well-being.

By connecting specific fingertips and your palms in various Mudra positions, you are directly affecting complex energy currents of your subtle energy body.
As numerous energy currents run thru your brain centers, Mudras help stimulate specific areas for an overall state of emotional, physical and mental well being.

Instructions for Mudra Practice

YOUR BODY POSTURE
During the Mudra practice sit in an upright position with a straight spine, with both your feet on the ground or in a cross legged position. Comfort is essential so that you may practice undisturbed and focus on proper practice positions.

YOUR EYES
Keep your eyes closed and gently lightly lift the gaze above the horizon.

WHERE
For achieving best results of ideal Mudra practice it is essential that you find a peaceful place, without distractions. Once your Mudra practice is established, you can practice Mudras anywhere.

WHEN

You may practice Mudras at any time. Best times for practice are first thing in the morning and at bedtime. Avoid practicing Mudras on a full stomach, and after a big meal wait for an hour before practice.

HOW LONG

Each Mudra should be practiced for at least 3 minutes at a time. Ideal practice is 3 Mudras for 3 minutes each with a follow up short 3 minutes of complete stillness, peace and meditation or reflection.

HOW OFTEN

You may practice Mudras every day. Explore various Mudras by selecting a Mudra that fits your specific needs for any given day.

Breath Control

Proper breathing is essential for optimal Mudra practice. There are two main breathing techniques that can be used with your practice.

LONG DEEP SLOW BREATH

Slowly and deeply inhale thru your nose while relaxing and expanding the area or your solar plexus and lower stomach. Exhale thru the nose slowly while gently contracting the stomach area and pulling your stomach in. Pace your breathing slowly and notice the immediate calming effects. This breathing technique is appropriate for relaxation, inducing calmness and peace.

BREATH OF FIRE

Inhale and exhale thru the nose at a much faster pace while practicing the same concept of expanding navel area and contracting with each exhalation. Unless otherwise noted Mudras are generally practiced with the long slow breath.The breath of fire has a energizing, recharging effect on body and is to be used only when so noted.

Chakras

Along our spine, starting at the base and continuing up towards the top of your head, lie subtle energy centers-vortexes-called charkas, that have a powerful effect on the overall state of your health and well being.
The practice of Mudras profoundly affects the proper function of these energy centers and magnifies their power.

Our subtle energy body is highly sensitive to outside sensory stimuli of sound, aromas, visuals and outside electric currents that constantly surround us. Frequencies that permeate specific locations may attract or bother you. Perhaps you may feel eager to stay somewhere where the energy suits you and yet feel suffocated when the environment does not agree with you. We are all sensitive to energies, but some of us feel them more than others.

A positive blend of energies with another person can create a magnet-like effect, whereas another person's negative unharmonious subtle energy field subconsciously pushes you away.

By leading healthy lives and optimizing the proper function of charkas, you empower your subtle energy bodies adding strength to your physical body, mind and spirit. Destructive behavior like addictions and abuse weakens your Auric field and "leaks" your vital energy. By maintaining a healthy Aura-energy field, you can fine-tune your natural capacity for "sensing" places, situations and people that compliment your energy frequency.
In a state of "clean energy" you achieve capacity for high awareness and become your own best guide.

Chakras in the body

Base Chakra: Foundation
Second Chakra: Sexuality
Third Chakra: Ego
Fourth Chakra: Love
Fifth Chakra: Truth
Sixth Chakra: Intuition
Seventh Chakra: Divine Wisdom

First Chakra

LOCATION: Base of the spine
GLAND: Gonad
COLOR: Red
REPRESENTS:
Foundation, shelter, survival,
courage, inner security, vitality

Second Chakra

LOCATION: Sex organs
GLAND: Adrenal
COLOR: Orange
REPRESENTS:
Creative expression, sexuality,
procreation, family

Third Chakra

LOCATION: Solar plexus
GLAND: Pancreas
COLOR: Yellow
REPRESENTS:
Ego, intellect, emotions of fear and anger

Fourth Chakra

LOCATION: Heart
GLAND: Thymus
COLOR: Green
REPRESENTS:
All matters of the heart, love,
self–love, compassion and faith

Fifth Chakra

LOCATION: Throat
GLAND: Thyroid
COLOR: Blue
REPRESENTS:
Communication, truth,
higher knowledge, your voice

Sixth Chakra

LOCATION: Third Eye
GLAND: Pineal
COLOR: Indigo
REPRESENTS:
Intuition, inner vision, the Third eye

Seventh Chakra

LOCATION: Top of the head - Crown
GLAND: Pituitary
COLOR: White and Violet
REPRESENTS:
The universal God consciousness,
the heavens, unity

Nadis

Your subtle energy body contains an amazing network of electric currents called Nadis. There are 72.000 energy currents that run throughout your body from toes to the top of your head as well as your fingertips. These channels of light must be clear and vibrant with life force for your optimal health and empowerment. With regular Mudra practice you can open, clear, reactivate and re-energize your energy currents.

Your Hands and Fingers

While practising Mudras you are magnifying the effects of the Solar system on your physical, mental and spiritual body. Each finger is influenced by the following planets:

THE THUMB - MARS

THE INDEX FINGER - JUPITER

THE MIDDLE FINGER- SATURN

THE RING FINGER – THE SUN

THE LITTLE FINGER- MERCURY

Mantra

Combining the Mudra practice with appropriate Mantras magnifies the beneficial effects of these ancient self-healing techniques.

The hard palate in your mouth has 58 energy meridian points that connect to and affect your entire body.

By singing, speaking or whispering Mantras, you touch these energy points in a specific order that is beneficial and has a harmonious and healing effect on your physical, mental and spiritual state.

The ancient science of Mantras helps you reactivate nadis, magnifies and empowers your energy field, improves your concentration and stills your mind.

About Astrology

The word Horoscope originates from a Latin word ORA–hour and SCOPOS–view. One could presume that Horoscope means "a look into your hour of birth". The precise moment of your birth determines your celestial set-up. An accurate astrological chart can reveal most detailed aspects of your life, your character, your gifts, your future possible events, challenges that await you, lucky events that are bestowed upon you, and your outlook for happy relationships, successful careers, accomplishments, health and many possible variations of life events. I say possible, because your decisions will determine the outcome.

There are 12 signs in the Zodiac and your birth-day reflects the position of your Sun sign. The specific positions of other planets in your chart are calculated considering the precise moment-hour and minute and of course location of your birth.

The birth time will reveal your Rising or Ascending sign, which will further determine other essential facts of your chart.

The constant transitional movements of the Planets affect each one of us differently, a time that may be difficult for some may prove supremely lucky for another and yet we are interconnected by mutual effects of continuous planetary movements. Nothing is standing still, the changes are ongoing.

On a different note, a few slow moving planets connect us in other ways, as they keep certain generations under specific aspects and influences.

We are all inseparable and in continuous motion.

There are numerous fascinating ways to use astrology and there is no doubt that the constant motion of all these powerful and majestic Planets in our Solar system affect each and every one of us differently.

Astrology can be used as an additional tool to help you continue progressing on the mysterious life journey of self discovery and self-realization.

Remember, the power of decision is yours as is the responsibility for consequences. Make peace with your doubts, pursue your dreams and relish in results.

When the outcome is less than what you expected, learn to pick yourself up and continue on, wiser with knowledge you gained, that alone being a good reason for remaining optimistic.

When the outcome surpasses your expectations, well, then you will know what to do…mostly take a breath, smile, and enjoy the moment.

Your Sun Sign

There are 12 signs in the Zodiac. The day of your birth determines your Sun-sign. Most often this is the extent of average person's knowledge and interest in astrology. However, the other aspects in the astrological chart are equally as important and need to be taken into consideration. In this book your main guide is your Sun sign's dispositions, tendencies, weaknesses and gifts. Certainly there are endless combinations of charts and your Sun sign alone will not reveal the complete picture of your celestial map.

For more detailed information and reflection about your chart, you need to know your ascending-rising sign.

Your Ascending-Rising Sign

Your rising sign, also known as the ascendant, reflects the degree of ecliptic rising over the eastern horizon at the precise moment of your birth. It reveals the foundation of your personality. That means that even if you have the same birthday with someone else, your time of birth would create completely different aspects and influences in your chart. No two people are alike. You are one of a kind and so is everyone else. However, you may have some strong similarities and timing aspects that will be often alike.

Your rising sign also reveals the basis of your chart and House placements. Your rising sign determines and is in your first house. There are 12 Houses and each depicts precise in-depth information about all aspects of your physical life, emotional make and character tendencies. It is incredibly complex and fascinating.

In regards to your Mudra practice in combination with your Astrological Sign, it would be beneficial to know also your Rising sign and apply Mudras that empower your Rising sign as well.

For example; if your Sun sign is Scorpio, but your rising sign is Libra-it would be most beneficial to practice Mudra sets for both signs.

How to use this book

In each book of the *Mudras for the Astrological Signs* series, you will find Mudras for different astrological signs that will help you in most important areas of your life: Health, Love, Success, and Overcoming your challenging qualities. We all have them, as we also all have gifts. This book is specific for the sign of Scorpio.

You may change your Mudra practice daily as needed, and keep in mind, that certain habits or tendencies need a longer time to adjust, change, and improve. Be patient, kind, and loving towards yourself.

Mudras for Transcending Challenges

Each one of us has a few character tendencies or weaknesses that are connected to our astrological chart. To help you transcend, overcome and redirect these challenges into your beneficial assets, you can use the Mudras in this chapter.

Mudras for Health and Beauty

Each astrological sign rules certain areas of your body. The Mudras in this chapter will help you strengthen your physical weaknesses while maintaining a healthy body, and a beautiful, vibrant appearance.

Mudras for Love

The Mudras in this chapter will help you understand your love temperament, your expectations, your longings and how to attract the optimal love partner into your life. It is most beneficial to know how others perceive you in the matters of the heart. It will also help you understand your partner and their astrologically influenced love map.

Mudras for Success

The Mudras in this chapter will offer you tools to present yourself to the world in your optimal light.
Often one is confused in which direction to turn or where their strength lies. Mudras will help you focus and remember your essential creative desires, help you gain self-confidence and inner security to recognize your desired and destined path. If you know what you want, and your purpose is harmonious for the better good of all, your success is within reach.

MUDRAS
for TRANSCENDING
CHALLENGES

MUDRA for
RELAXATION and JOY

Your intense and competitive nature pushes you into overdrive. Your deep, complex, and analysing mind needs down time filled with peace and solitude. Make it a point to schedule regular relaxation times for yourself where you can rejuvenate and refresh, so that you are ready and enthusiastic to return to your projects with renewed energy. This Mudra is an excellent tool for you to let go and learn to spend some easy and peaceful time with yourself.

CHAKRA : 3, 4

COLOR: Yellow, green

MANTRA:

HAREE HAR HAREE HAR
(God in His Creative Aspect)

Sit with a straight back, lift up your hands up in front of your chest. Make a fist with your left hand, tucking the thumb inside. Wrap the right hand around the left and place your right thumb over the base of the left thumb. Concentrate on your third Eye area and hold for three minutes. With time, extend your practice to eleven minutes.

BREATH:
Long, deep and slow.

MUDRA for

PROTECTION

You are secretive and get fascinated by the darker side of this world. You feel you can play with fire and nothing will ever happen to you. Invincible and indestructible. Often your curiosity will get the best of you and you may find yourself caught or even trapped in a dangerous place or habit. Call upon the Divine power to protect and guide you at all times. Practice this Mudra and consciously select a wiser path. Life can be just as adventurous without careless danger.

CHAKRA : All

COLOR: All

MANTRA:

OM
(God in His Absolute State)

Sit with a straight spine. Cross your left hand over
your right one and place them on your upper
chest. Palms are facing you and all fingers are
together. Hold for three minutes and feel the
immediate energy shift.

BREATH:
Long, deep and slow.

MUDRA
for EMPOWERING
Your VOICE

Just like the scorpion can sting with an unexpected bite, so can you with your sharp words. Fearless in conflict or confrontations, your sarcastic capacity can wound a more sensitive and delicate person. Transcending your power into a state of higher awareness and guiding your counterpart towards a spiritual realization will bring you more happiness, inner fulfilment, and better karma. Practice this Mudra when you are tempted to "sting", and overcome this hurtful urge. Your natural magnetism will charm your opponent and disarm them completely.

CHAKRA: 5

COLOR: Blue

Sit with a straight back, bend your elbows and lift
them parallel to the ground, while you lift your
hands in front of you at the level of your throat.
Turn the right palm outward and the left palm
towards you. Bend your fingers and hook your
palms together, while pulling them apart.
Keep your shoulders down while
applying pressure to the pull.

BREATH:
Long deep and slow.

MUDRAS
for HEALTH
and BEAUTY

MUDRA for Overcoming ADDICTIONS

Your fascination with the darker underworld sometimes seduces you into a self destructive pattern. You may think you are invincible for a while, but do not let careless experiments get the best of you. Your physical body has a certain stamina, but overindulgence is a trait you must overcome with focus and intention. We learn from all our experiences and so will you. Your sign has the amazing capacity to rise from the ashes of a burning, destructive fire, and experience a true rebirth. Next time, you are hopefully older and wiser. Practice this Mudra when you feel the pull of the darker side and truly prove yourself that you are stronger than your temptations.

CHAKRA : 1, 2,3, 4, 5

COLOR: Red, orange, yellow, green, blue

Sit with a straight back. Make fists with both hands
and then extend the thumbs out. Press the thumbs
on the temples where you feel a slight depression.
Clench your teeth, lock the back molars, and keep
your lips closed. Vibrate the jaw muscles by
alternating the pressure on the molars. A muscle will
move in rhythm under the thumbs. Feel it massage
the thumbs as you continue to apply firm pressure
with them. Concentrate on your Third eye area as
you do this. Continue for three to eleven minutes.
Now relax your arms and place them at your sides,
with the thumbs and index fingers forming a circle.
Hold and relax.

BREATH:
Long, deep and slow.

MUDRA for

Balancing SEXUAL Energy

Your sign rules sex organs and you are most likely
a deeply sensual and sexual being. However, you
do know that anything in excess can attract
disharmony. Therefore it is wise that you take extra
precaution and learn to balance your drive so that
you are the one in charge. Keep in mind that simply
following your desires does not guarantee
happiness and after you fixate on your conquest,
take a moment and truly reflect if this pursuit is
worth it. If it is just a compulsive habit, take a step
back and go deeper within yourself. The fulfilment
you so desire requires a multi-layered satisfaction.
And remember, every time you physically merge
with someone, you blend the energy fields of the
two and carry this specific frequency with you for
quite a while. So be selective and protective.
This Mudra will help you redirect
your sexual nature to a healthy place.

CHAKRA : 2

COLOR: Orange

Sit with a straight back, elbows slightly out to the side. Clasp your hands together, interlocking your fingers. Leave the left little finger outside of the hand. By placing the right thumb on top of the left thumb we empower our masculine side, and when the left thumb is placed on top of the right thumb we recharge the feminine side of our nature. Press your hands together in this Mudra, hold for three minutes and relax.

BREATH:
Long, deep and slow.

MUDRA for
Preventing BURNOUT

Living wild and living fast can have its price. Be who you are and enjoy every minute of it, but give your body enough down time to recover so that you can stay happy and healthy. This applies especially your non stop work ethics or extreme adventure sports. Know your limits and consciously assess the dangers and risks taken. A good approach is a planned even distribution of your energy and awareness of your stamina. Do not overexert yourself. This Mudra will help you preserve and recharge your vital energy.

CHAKRA : 1, 2 ,3

COLOR: Red, yellow, orange

MANTRA:

OM
(God in His Absolute State)

Sit with a straight back. Bring your forearms up in front of you at heart level and bend your elbows to the side. With the palms facing the ground, fold your thumbs across the palms of each hand till they reach the bases of your ring fingers. Now bend your fingers slightly and touch the backs of your fingertips together, forming a V-shape with your hands. Hold for three minutes and make sure your elbows remain elevated.

BREATH:
Long, deep and slow.

MUDRAS
for LOVE

MUDRA for
Sixth Chakra-TRUTH

In every love relationship honesty is a key component for harmony. Keeping secrets is limiting the level to which your love can grow. There is always a slight guard to keep and a distance is created. Give it a try and learn that when you are honest, you will enjoy the same quality in return. You are a mirror to your partner and everything that you see and do not like, you can find in yourself as well. The discontent that will overcome your relationship when you are burdened with secrets, may prove detrimental. This Mudra will help you overcome the tendency to "modify the truth" and truly feel free and merge with your partner.

CHAKRA: 6

COLOR: Violet

MANTRA:
EK ONG KAR
(One Creator, God is One)

Sit with a straight back. Bend your elbows and lift your arms up so that the elbows are parallel to the ground. Palms are facing out and all fingers are together. Hold for there minutes.

BREATH:
Long, deep and slow.

MUDRA for TRUST

The issue with trust is far from simple,
but honestly answering this question may help:
how much do you trust yourself?
When you get jealous, suspicious and possessive,
could it be possible that the situations you are
connecting to your partner in reality apply to you?
Do you have those habits? Could it be that knowing
what you are capable of drives you mad and you are
just venting? Here we are again back to honesty
and truth. When you settle down and face your
demons, know and understand why you
have pursued something that may have jeopardized
your true happiness at home, then the problem will
vanish into the thin air. This Mudra will help you
learn how to trust yourself and others. Most of all;
trust the Divine power to always guide you into the
right direction. Keep that channel clear.

CHAKRA: 7

COLOR: Violet

MANTRA:
HAR HAR HAR WAHE GURU
(God's Creation, His Supreme power and Wisdom)

Sit with a straight back. Make a circle with
your arms arched up over your head, palms down.
Put the right palm on top of the left.
Lightly press the thumb tips together,
keep your back straight and visualize a
circle of white protective light around you.

BREATH:
Short, fast, breath of fire focusing on the navel.
Practice for a minute and relax with deep
slow breath for another two minutes.

MUDRA for

POWERFUL SPEECH

Gentle words are soothing to the heart, healing the sorrow and nurturing to your lover. That is what we all desire to hear. Before you thoughtlessly say something you did not mean, take a breath and decide what is it you want to achieve as a result. If it is love and romance, then you, better than anyone, can create that sensual environment with words alone. If you want to hurt your lover in a stressful impulsive moment, take a step back and be wise. Each time you succumb to that urge, the love will be chipped away a bit. Not worth it, for your lover is yours alone. Be confident and communicate your passionate, powerful magnetism properly-with deeply profound love that you are capable of. This Mudra will help you remember how to embellish your words with seductive loving honey.

CHAKRA: 5

COLOR: Blue

Sit with a straight back. Place your hands in front of your chest, palms apart and all fingertips touching. All fingers are spread apart. Inhale and press together the thumbs and the index fingers. Exhale and relax. Now inhale and press together the thumbs and the middle fingers. Exhale and relax.
Continue the same way with the ring and little fingers. Practice for three minutes and finish up the cycle.

BREATH:
Long, deep and slow.

MUDRAS
for SUCCESS

MUDRA for
CALMING Your MIND

Your mind is on fire and the tendency can wear you out. You definitely have a competitive streak and when someone in the same profession near you does well, you will notice it and it will affect you. The best way to navigate this disposition is to use this a as stimulant to strive to get better and more successful. Remember that success comes in many ways and definitions and thoroughly reflect what is it really that you wish for. Be the master of your mind and you will become the master of your life. This Mudra will help you achieve the state of inner calm and peace. And that is an essential element for finding a balance and a successful, prosperous career.

CHAKRA: 3, 4, 6

COLOR: Yellow, Green, indigo

MANTRA:
OM
(God in His Absolute State)

Sit with a straight spine. Cross your arms in front
of your chest, elbows are bend and at a ninety
degree angle. Arms are parallel to the ground.
Place the right palm on top of the left arm and the
the top of the left hand under the right arm.
All fingers are together and straight.
Hold and keep the elbows nice and high.

BREATH:
Long, deep and slow.

MUDRA for WISDOM

Wise choices and wise decisions are part of the perfect plan to your success. Recognizing when something may not be the most positive experience for you and watching over your wild inner nature is what this Mudra will help you achieve. Make sure that your pursuits are motivated wisely and not just with pure emotion and passion. Use your intensity to magnify your natural power and there will be no limitations to what you can do and achieve. Inner wisdom can be awakened, heard and empowered when you wisely decide to do so.
It is never too late or too early.
The prefect time is now.

CHAKRA : 6

COLOR: Indigo

MANTRA:
SAT NAM
(Truth Is God's Name, One in Spirit)

Sit with a straight spine and bend your elbows to the side, parallel to the ground. Make gentle fists, with the thumbs inside and the index fingers out. Now hook your index fingers around each other. The right palm is facing down and the left toward your chest.

BREATH:
Long, deep and slow.

MUDRA for
RELEASING Negativity

Your passionate nature can sometimes get
dramatically discouraged when things don't go your
way. But remember that every successful person
failed many times before and certainly you would
not want to give up. When you feel the competitive
nature wallowing in jealousy if another person is
winning, practice this Mudra and breathe out all that
may not be positive. Consciously decide that all you
want to carry around is positivity, love, passion,
honesty and your immense inner power.
Then you will become the true winner
that you were born to be.

CHAKRA: 4

COLOR: Green

Sit with a straight back. Bend your arms and
make fists with both hands. Bring them up in
front of your heart. Cross the hands over
each other, palms turned outwards.
Hold the Mudra across the chest
with the left arm on the outer side.

BREATH:
Long, deep and slow.

ABOUT THE AUTHOR

SABRINA MESKO Ph.D.H. is the LA Times and international bestselling author of *Healing Mudras -Yoga for your Hands* by Random House. Her book reached number five on the Los Angeles Times Health Books Bestseller list and is translated into 14 languages. Her other books include *Power Mudras, YOGA MIND, Mudra Cards* by Andrews McMeel, *Mudra- Gestures of Power* and more. She produced and directed her Visionary awards finalist double DVD titled *Chakra Mudras*.

Sabrina studied with Master Guru Maya, healing breath techniques with Master Sri Sri Ravi Shankar and completed a four-year study of Paramahansa Yogananda's Kriya Yoga technique. She graduated from Yoga College of India and became a certified yoga therapist. An immense interest and study of powerful hand gestures-Mudras, led Sabrina to the world's only Master of White Tantric Yoga, Yogi Bhajan, who entrusted her with the sacred Mudra - hand yoga techniques giving her the responsibility to spread this ancient and powerful knowledge world wide.

Sabrina holds a Bachelors Degree in Sensory Approaches to Healing, a Masters in Holistic Science and a Doctorate in Ancient and Modern Approaches to Healing from the American Institute of Holistic Theology. She is board certified from the American Alternative medical Association and American Holistic Health Association. Sabrina appeared on The Discovery Channel documentary on hands, the Roseanne Show, CNBC News and numerous international live television programs. Her articles and columns have been published in countless publications. Sabrina has hosted her own weekly TV show about health, well-being and complementary medicine. She is an executive member of the World Yoga Council and has led extensive Teacher Training Yoga Therapy educational programs. Sabrina has also created award winning international Spa and Wellness Centers from concept, architectural planning, equipment and product selection, staff training and unique healing signature Spa treatments. She is a motivational keynote conference speaker addressing large audiences all over the world. Her highly dynamic and engaging approach leaves audiences inspired and uplifted. Sabrina lives in Los Angeles. For more information about her online personal mentorship courses for MUDRA TEACHER TRAINING and MUDRA THERAPY visit her website: **www.sabrinamesko.com**

Made in the USA
Monee, IL
30 May 2021

69746238R00035